Praise!

Praise!

Songs and poems from the Bible
retold for children

by

A. J. McCallen

Illustrations by
Ferelith Eccles Williams

COLLINS

North American Edition
Published by
Servant Books
P.O. Box 8617
Ann Arbor, Michigan 48107
ISBN 0-89283-107-3

First Published 1979
Reprinted 1980

Made and printed by
William Collins Sons & Co Ltd
Glasgow

CONTENTS

Trust Him!

Ask Him!

Listen to Him!

Thank Him!

INTRODUCTION

The Book of Praise shows us how we can turn to God our Father and pray to him in good times and in bad times:

to praise him for his greatness
to remember his goodness
to get to know both his gentleness and his strength
to trust in his love
to ask for his help
to listen to his teaching
to thank him for his kindness.

I hope these poems and prayers will help you to get to know God our Father better and to love him.

A. J. MCCALLEN

Praise Him!

1

It's good to know how great God the Father is.

Clap your hands and shout for joy.
God is King of all the earth!

Play the trumpet loud and clear.
God is King of all the earth!

Sing and praise him, everyone.
God is King of all the earth!

Praise him now with all your skill.
God is King of all the earth!

2

Look all around the world.
See how many wonderful things there are.
They are beautiful, they are marvellous
—they give praise to God the Father.

The sun and the moon praise God
   the shining stars adore him.
Snow and hail praise God
   and the mighty winds that obey him.

The depths of the sea praise God
   and all the monsters of the ocean.
The birds in the sky praise God
   and even the snakes that crawl on the ground.

All the animals of the world praise God
   both wild and tame.
The hills and mountains praise God
   and all the trees.

The Kings of the earth praise God
   and all their peoples.
Men and women praise God
   both young and old.

Let everyone praise our God
   for he is wonderful.
Let everyone praise the living God
   for he is the Lord of heaven and earth.

3

*God the Father does so many things so very well
we simply* have *to praise him.*

How many stars are in the sky?
—God knows exactly.
He even knows the names of each of them
because he made them.

Our God is powerful,
our God is wise.
Praise him!

He spreads the clouds across the sky
and makes the rain fall.
He makes the grass grow in the fields
and feeds the animals.

Our God is powerful,
our God is wise.
Praise him!

The little ravens call to him
when they are hungry.
He will feed and care for them
and protect them.

Our God is powerful,
our God is wise.
Praise him!

The snow falls down as thick as cotton wool
—because he says so!
He scatters frost upon the earth
—like talcum powder!
He fires hail stones from the sky
—like bullets!
Then just as suddenly
he sends the winds to blow away the ice
and melt the rivers!

Our God is powerful,
our God is wise.
Praise him!

16

4

God the Father gives us beautiful trees
and keeps them alive in summer and winter.
That's one very good reason to praise him.
He also keeps us alive as well
and makes us strong
—and that's even better!

Down by the river
is a good place for trees.
If the water flows near them,
they never grow dry.
Their leaves are not withered,
they stay green and alive.
And each year their branches
are covered with fruit.

The man that is good
is like a tree by the river.
God will look after him;
God will protect him
—like a tree by the river
he will grow strong!

5

God is not poor
he is richer than we can ever imagine
for everything belongs to him!
Blessed be God!

Whenever you see the animals in the woods
remember they belong to me.

Whenever you see the cattle on the hillsides
remember who made them.

Whenever you see the birds up on the treetops
remember I know each one of them.

Whenever you see a living thing out in the fields
think of me.

6

God the Father does the most wonderful, the most clever things
—he even makes us!
That's why we praise him with all our hearts.

Before I was born,
you made each little part of me in secret.

While I was hidden in my mother's womb,
you watched me grow.
You saw my bones begin to form
and join together.

From the first moment of my life
you knew me!

I praise you, Lord,
and I am filled with wonder.
For everything you do
is strange and marvellous.

7

God the Father is never far away
—he loves us too much
to leave us all on our own.
That's why we praise him!

You know me, Lord, so very well,
you know when I get up.
You know when I go back to sleep,
you know each thing I do.

You know what I am going to say
before I even speak!
You are *always* close to me.
You're wonderful, O Lord.

So if I climb the highest hill,
you would be there with me.
And if I swam beneath the waves,
you'd still be there with me.

Even in the dark at night
you would be next to me.
Yes, even then I could not hide,
you would be there with me.

8

God is so big and so strong
—and yet he is so gentle and loving
to even the smallest of us.
That's why we praise him!

I look up at the stars
high in the sky
—how small *we* are
   in this beautiful world!
And yet you love us.

You have made us like yourself
—the Kings of the Earth
   to care for the animals wild and tame
   and the birds in the air
   and the fish in the sea.

You are so great
and so good!

9

Jesus says:
God really is faithful and loving.
That's why we praise him.

ALL of your people shall praise you, O Lord,
   BLESSED BE GOD!
BECAUSE you are faithful and loving and good.
   BLESSED BE GOD!
CAN anyone else be as strong as the Lord?
   BLESSED BE GOD!
DOES anyone else do such wonderful deeds?
   BLESSED BE GOD!
EVERYONE turns to the Lord God for help,
   BLESSED BE GOD!
FOR HE is the King who takes care of us all.
   BLESSED BE GOD!
GIVE praise to the Lord God for ever and ever!
   BLESSED BE GOD!

10

God our Father is very good to us.
That's why we are glad to praise him!

God is very good to us.
  Let's praise him.

Let's play the trumpet.
  Let's praise him.

Let's play the guitar.
  Let's praise him.

Let's play the drums.
  Let's praise him.

Let's play the violins.
  Let's praise him.

Let's play the recorders.
  Let's praise him.

Let's crash the cymbals.
  Let's praise him.

Let's dance for joy.
  Let's praise him.

Let everyone who can breathe
  PRAISE GOD!

11

Jesus says
'God is my Father.
Praise him for he is your Father also.'

Lord God,
how great you are.
Everything you have done is wonderful.
You are the King of the whole wide world.

Who will not praise you!
Who will not thank you!
You are God, the Holy One!
Everyone will come and worship you
for everyone can see what you have done.

Remember Him!

12

God, of course, loves everyone,
and he wants everyone to be happy with him.
This is why he chose Abraham's family
to be his own special People—
so that they could tell everyone else about him.
The family of Abraham never forgot God's kindness to them.

Give thanks to the Lord for he is great!
Tell everyone what he has done
Be glad that he has made us his own People.

He is the Lord.
He is our God.
We *know* we can trust him
for *he* keeps his promises!

Remember the promise
  he once made to Abraham.
Remember the promise
  he once made to Isaac.
Remember the promise
  he once made to Jacob long, long ago.
I WILL GIVE YOU A COUNTRY,
YOUR VERY OWN COUNTRY,
TO BE YOUR OWN HOME.

But long, long ago
we were not a Great People,
we were only poor wanderers.
Yet God still stood by us
for we were *his* People!

So when the crops withered
    and there was a famine
    and people were hungry,
it was God who sent Joseph
    as a slave into Egypt,
and God who put Joseph
    in charge of the country
    as the King's right-hand man!

Then the People all joined him
    and stayed there in Egypt
    with all of their children,
till the People of Egypt
    were scared by their numbers
    and started to hate them
    and made them their slaves.

But God raised up Moses
   to care for his People
and showed the Egyptians
   the power of his strength!
God made the daylight
   as dark as the night-time
   all over Egypt!
He poisoned their rivers
   and made their fish die!
Sent frogs in their hundreds
   and black clouds of insects,
and hailstones for rain
   that smashed down their vines!
Thousands of locusts
   ate up their cornfields,
and even their children grew sick
   and then died!

But he led out *his* People
   all safe and healthy.
He led them to safety
   right through the desert
with a cloud in the day-time
   to give them protection
and a fire in the night-time
   to light up their way!
When they were hungry
   he sent quails every evening
   and food straight from heaven
   and water to drink!

He remembered that promise
   he once made to Abraham.
He gave us our country
   and made it our home.

That's why we praise him
FOR HE IS OUR GOD!

13

The People of God had many great leaders over the years,
but the greatest King they ever had
was the famous King David.
He was the one they remembered best of all.

God led his People to a Promised Land
to a special place that he had won for them.

And yet they all forgot what he had done.
They even turned their backs on him
and followed other gods.
That was why they suffered such disasters!

But still God did not leave them helpless as they were.
It was as if he woke up suddenly from sleep
and came and rescued them.

Then the Lord chose David as their King.
He picked him out from looking after sheep,
and made him Shepherd of his People.
He chose him as the Leader of his People
and David guided them with loving care and skill.

14

*The People of God never forgot that he had chosen them to be his
   People.*
But they did not always do what God told them to do.
Sometimes it was only when they were in serious trouble
that they began to think about him again.
*Then they remembered how he had looked after them with loving
   care*
*—just as a gardener looks after a special kind of vine that he has
   planted in his garden.*

Remember long ago, Lord God,
how you saw a little vine
in a country far away.
Remember how you chose it for your garden
and brought it down from Egypt
to this country.
Remember how you cleared the ground for it,
how you chose a special place for it to grow.

That vine grew strong
and grew deep roots.
It grew so tall
it stretched above the tallest trees
and spread throughout the countryside
from the valleys to the mountain tops
until it covered all the hillsides with its shadow
from the Great Wide River to the Sea!

But now look what has happened to that vine!
All the fences round your vineyard have been broken.
Anyone can come and steal your grapes.
Your enemies have cut down all its branches
set fire to them
and burnt the vines!

The big wild pigs rush in to eat the fruit
and stamp on everything in front of them!

Lord God,
remember how you planted this, your vineyard.
Remember how you cared for the smallest vines.
Remember how you made it grow so tall and strong . . .

AND COME AGAIN AND SAVE YOUR VINEYARD
 NOW!

15

The People of God were captured by their enemies
and made to live in a country far away.
It was a long time before they could come home again,
and when they did, they found everything had been spoilt.
They had to begin all over again.

In good times and bad times
we can always trust God.

It seemed like a dream
when we all came back home
to the Old Country.
We laughed and we sang
for God was so good to us.

In good times and bad times
we can always trust God.

But then we found the river beds were dry.
The land was hard and overgrown.
And many of us cried
when we tried to plant seeds
in the hard dry soil.

In good times and bad times
we can always trust God.

But now it's harvest time
and all the people who were crying then
are laughing now,
carrying in great sheaves of golden wheat
singing for joy!

In good times and bad times
we can always trust God.

16

Long ago there was a 'Temple' in Jerusalem
—a beautiful church surrounded by splendid courtyards.
This poem was obviously written by a person who loved to
come and pray in the temple,
and now he looks back and remembers
what it was like to be there.

Lord God, I love your Temple.
If only I could be there now!
One day spent in the Temple courtyards
is better than a thousand anywhere else!

I can see the little sparrows
building their nests high up on the walls.
I can picture the swallows
feeding their young beside the altar.
How lucky they are to be so close to you,
praising you each day with all their songs!

I can imagine the groups of travellers
eager to come and see Jerusalem
coming down the valley from the Desert
into a land of sweet, fresh pools of water.

Lord God,
you are our King.
It is good to put our trust in you!

17

We remember Abraham, Moses and King David long ago.
We also remember Jesus who is our *Saviour.*
He is the Son of God who shows us *how to live.*
He is the one who sets us *free.*

Praise the Lord
for he has come
and visited his People.
God has sent a Saviour who is strong
and he will set us free.

He promised this to Abraham so long ago,
and he has kept his word.
He promised he would make us free from fear
and safe from harm.
Then we could live in peace with him for ever.

John the Baptist walked before the Lord.
He prepared the way for him to go.
He was the man who showed us Christ had come
—come to forgive us all our sins.

God is gentle, God is kind:
he leads us from the dark
so that the brightness of his light
can shine upon us all day long
and guide us on the way of peace.

Get to Know Him!

18

If we know anything at all about God,
we will know he is someone who takes good care of us.
God our Father is someone we can trust.

Blessed be God!
He listens to me.
He hears me,
when I pray for help.

Blessed be God!

I trust the Lord,
for he is strong.
I thank the Lord,
for he takes care of me.

Blessed be God!

19

Something else about God our Father
—he is a person who will be gentle and kind with us.

We don't mind
even if the earth shakes
even if the sea is raging.
Even if the hills fall down
we don't mind!

God is like the gentle river
that flows beside the House of Prayer
bringing water to our city
to make us strong
and make us glad.

God lives with us
in our own city.
Whatever happens
we are safe.

Come and see the great things God can do.
Everywhere he stops the people fighting
—he breaks their bows
—he snaps their spears
—he burns their shields.

Stop all your fighting now—he says
and come to me.
I am the Lord of the whole wide world.
Listen to what I have to say:
Be still
and come to me.
I am your God.

20

We know we are safe with God our Father.

At night I lie in bed
and think of you, Lord God.
I lie there in the darkness of the night
and remember how good you are,
for you have always helped me.

I am like a little bird
that clings to its mother.
You are like the mighty eagle
who spreads its wings above its young
to protect them.

I am happy to lie here in the dark
under the shadow of your wings, Lord God.

21

God is gentle—yes certainly.
But God our Father is also a God of strength and might
—as strong as the crashing waves and the mighty wind.

Listen to the sound of water
of waves crashing on the rocks.
Listen to the sound of thunder
far away, far out at sea . . .

and you will hear the voice of God.

Listen to the sound of trees
groaning, creaking in the storm.
Listen to them crack and break . . .

and you will hear the voice of God.

Listen to the hissing desert winds
that sweep the sand along the valley
making all the land begin to tremble . . .

and you will hear the voice of God.

Glory be to God!
the people cry,
many voices joined together
singing in the House of Prayer,
praising God, their Lord and King.

22

Don't think God our Father is 'soft'!
He is powerful and strong.

God is . . .

as strong as an earthquake
that shakes the whole world
and makes the mountains tremble!

as strong as a volcano
that splits the land open
pouring out fire
and burning flames
and clouds of smoke!

God is . . .

as powerful as a thunderstorm at night
when everything is dark
and lightning 'flashes' across the sky
cutting through the heavy rain clouds
like an arrow!

when the mighty sound of thunder
rumbles overhead
like a deep and angry roar!

23

God is so great, so important
you would hardly expect him to think about us at all.
But he does!

Look up at the sun
and remember God is brighter still!

Look up at the sky
and remember it is nothing more than a little tent
in front of God!

The clouds that glide across the sky
are like chariots for God to ride in!

The rushing winds
merely blow against his feet!

24

Long ago people used to worship statues and totem poles.
We know God our Father is someone much bigger
than anything like that.
He is the God of all the world!

The pagans worship idols made of gold.
How stupid!
Idols made of gold are not alive.
They're only made by human hands. That's all!

They have a mouth,
but cannot speak!
They have two eyes,
but cannot see!
They have two ears,
but cannot hear!
They have a nose,
but cannot breathe!

How stupid.
They're not much use at all!

25

Just think of it—God made us!
We know that for certain.
How wonderful he must be!

People say
'We can do what we want.
God can't see us.
He won't take any notice!'

How can they be so stupid!
Won't they ever learn at all!

God *made* our ears
—so surely he can *hear!*

God *made* our eyes
—so surely he can *see!*

God is the greatest teacher in the world
—so surely he can *understand.*
He even knows the secret thoughts we think!

26

Sometimes other people let us down—even our closest friends!
God our Father will never do this.
That's one thing we can know for certain.

My best friend has wounded me
and broken all his promises.
He pretended to be good to me
when really he was full of hate.
He pretended to be kind to me
but deep down he was hard and cruel.

I wouldn't mind if he had always been my enemy,
but he was once my closest friend!
—*We* were always friends together
and shared our secrets.

I sometimes wish that I was like a bird
with wings
—like a dove,
then I would fly away
and find somewhere to rest
far away in the desert
in a sheltered place
where I could be safe from all the cruel winds,
safe from all the people who can hurt me.

27

We know we can stay close
to God our Father, safe and secure.

It was dark.
It was night-time
and the birds were all resting.

Then along came a man with a bow.
He drew his bow tight
and took aim with an arrow
to shoot and to kill!

But as soon as they heard him
the birds flew to safety
to the far-away mountains.

*   *   *   *

You are foolish to say
'Fly away like the birds!'

I won't fly away
when people attack me.
I trust in the Lord
and I will be safe.

I know he can see me
—he can see everybody.
He knows who is good
and he knows who is bad.

Because *he* is good,
he loves to see goodness,
he hates to see violence.
So we can be sure
if we do what is right
we can live close beside him
safe and secure.

28

Mary, the mother of Jesus, put her trust in God.
She knew she could trust him.

I praise the Lord for he is good.
He makes me glad!
I am young and I am poor,
and yet he comes and chooses me!
And from now on,
everyone will say that he has blessed me.

The Lord is strong, the Lord is generous,
stretching out his hand to help the sick,
feeding hungry people with good food,
looking after people everywhere!

Long ago he said that he would help us.
Now the Lord has kept his promise perfectly!
He has not forgotten his own People.
He has come to rescue them
and keep them safe!

Trust Him!

29

*Again and again the Book of Praise says,
'You can always trust God'.*

I saw a mother
carrying her baby
in her arms
so gently
so quietly.

I am at peace
like that baby
and I am happy
—*I trust in God.*

30

*You can trust in God
even when everything else lets you down!*

The soldiers are proud
of their glittering chariots
and the speed of their horses.
But even *their* horses
can stumble and fall
—and when they fall down
   they're no use at all!

We don't trust in horses.
We trust in God.
He will take care of us.

He will take care of us better than horses,
for when we fall down
he will help us stand up
and stand firm.

31

All sorts of different people put their trust in God
—the sailors for example.

Sailors know the mighty strength of God.
They travel everywhere in ships
across the Oceans of the world,
and they have seen the winds begin to blow
whipping up the water out at sea
lifting up their ships high in the air
and dashing them back down into the depths.

Even sailors can become afraid
when they begin to stagger up on deck
like drunken men!
They know how to turn to God in danger.
He can change the storm to perfect stillness
and bring them safely home again to harbour.

32

Sometimes when people do wrong, they feel cold and miserable
—like someone who is all alone and very lonely
    in the darkness of the night.
But God our Father doesn't want people to be all alone like that.
He wants them to know they can trust him
—he will come and help them.

The watchman waits at dead of night
waiting for the dawn
waiting for the sun to rise.

Everything is dark and cold,
but soon the brightness of the dawn
will fill the murky sky with daylight!

The watchman knows—the dawn *will* come.

*   *   *   *

I am waiting in the dead of night,
waiting in the darkness
waiting for the Lord to come.

'Forgive me, Lord,
I have done wrong.'

I long for you to come to me
to take away the darkness of my sins,
for you are loving and forgiving
—you are like the brightness of the sun
    that comes to light up all the world each morning.

Like the watchman
I am sure that you will come,
and you will listen to my prayer.

52

33

*God our Father is like a shepherd
who takes good care of all his sheep.*

The shepherd takes good care of all his sheep
and they have everything they need.
He knows a green and grassy field
beside a pool of clear water
and he leads his sheep to eat and rest
in safety there,
and they grow strong.

He knows the mountain tracks by day and night,
and with his shepherd's crook
he guides the sheep along the way.
Even in the darkness of the night-time
his sheep are not afraid
for he is with them.

The Lord has always been The Shepherd of his People.
He feeds them with a banquet of rich food and drink
and they grow strong.
He pours upon their heads the oil of gladness,
for he is good and loving to them always
and they can stay in safety with him all their lives.

34

We are safe with God

Lord,
you look after me.
I am safe with you.

Lord, I am safe with you.

I go to bed at night
and fall asleep
and nothing worries me.

Lord, I am safe with you.

I wake up safe and sound
for *you* protect me.

Lord, I am safe with you.

35

*The Followers of Jesus know they can trust God the Father
   always.*

I dreamed the world was all stretched out in front of me,
but now it was *made new*.
I saw the City where the people lived,
but now it seemed like part of heaven.

I heard a loud voice
and it said,
'God has come to live with men!
He has made his home with them.
They will be his chosen People.
He will be their loving God.

'He will wipe away the tears from their eyes.
He will put an end to suffering.
There will be no more of all this sadness.
There will be no more of all this crying.
There will be no more of all this pain.
Trust God.'

Ask Him!

36

God doesn't really fall asleep!
The Book of Praise is only telling us
*   that we can always ask God to help us.*
and especially when we're all upset and confused.

Wake up, God!
Don't say you're still sleeping!
Can't you see we need you?
So please don't hide away.
Look, we're all in trouble.
Don't forget us please.

Wake up, God, and hear us!
Show us that you love us.
Come and help us now.

37

Things go wrong; people hurt us; we feel upset.
Even then, we can always ask God to listen
—he will hear us.

I cry myself to sleep each night
worn out with tears,
my eyes so red and swollen
I can hardly see.

Lord, I am crying.
Come and rescue me.

38

Sometimes people are so ill
  that there is very little anyone else can do to help.
This man feels like that.

My life is burning away
like the smoke that curls up from the dying fire.
My body is hot and feverish.
I cannot eat.

I cry out loud
like some animal in the desert
like an owl in the wilderness.

All night long I lie awake
like the little bird up on the house-top.

I am withering away like the grass!

Listen to my prayer, O Lord.
Listen to my cry for help.
Come quickly.

39

Sometimes God seems to be miles away
and we feel all alone.
But that's not really true.
God is really very close to us.
It's just that we don't always notice him.

Father,
you seem to be so far away!
Why have you left me on my own?
Come quickly and help me.

You are so good.
You have always helped your people.
They trusted you
and you have never let them down.

40

Here is a prayer written by a man who nearly drowned!
He is scared stiff and prays to God for help.

Save me, O God, I'm drowning!
The water is up to my neck!
I'm standing on soft oozy mud
and my feet are beginning to sink.
I cannot stand up
for the waves push me down,
and the water is getting still deeper!

Save me, O God, I'm drowning!
The mud is sinking below me,
the water is pushing me over!
Save me or I will die!

41

Sometimes when people do wrong,
they feel so ashamed of themselves
that they feel bad in themselves.
They feel all 'broken up'.
Sometimes the only way to feel better again
is to own up to what is wrong
and to ask God to sort things out
—like the man in this prayer.

I am crushed with sadness.
I feel as if my bones are broken.
For I have sinned against my loving Lord.
I have done wrong.

Don't look at me, O Lord.
Please shut your eyes.
You mustn't see what I have done!

Come and wash away the blackness of my sins
and make me clean
—as clean as snow.

I know that I have sinned.
I can't forget it!
I have sinned against you.
I have done wrong in front of you, my God.

Come and help me, Lord.
Come and rescue me.
Fill me with your happiness and joy
and make me come alive again.

62

42

This is the story of a soldier
left on the battlefield
by his friends who thought he was dead.
But now the enemy have found him, helpless,
  lying alone in the mud!

My enemies are like a herd of bulls
standing around me,
like big angry bulls
all ready to attack!
Like so many lions
with huge open mouths
roaring with anger
and ready to bite!

I've become like a worm
and everyone hates me.
Everyone sneers at me
sticking out their tongues
and shaking their heads,
AND NO ONE WILL STOP THEM!

I'm hopelessly weak.
I've no strength at all.
I'm as helpless as water
poured out on the ground.
My bones have been broken
and put out of joint.
My heart is like hot wax
that burns deep inside me.
My throat is so dry
it's as dry as the dust,
and my tongue is stuck tight
to the roof of my mouth!

Yet still they surround me
like packs of wild dogs!
They rip off my clothes
to keep for themselves,
and play 'heads and tails'
to see who gets my cloak.
They tear at my skin
at my hands and my feet
till my bare bones are showing!

Lord,
come and help me.
Don't wait far away!
Come and save me
from these dogs
from these lions
from these wild beasts!
I AM HELPLESS ON MY OWN.

43

*It's good to know that God is ready to help us
especially when we fall down,
like Peter when he sank in the lake.*

I was slipping,
I was falling,
I could not help myself,
as I fell into that deep and oozy pit!
Help me, Lord!

The Lord bent down
and he pulled me up.
He heard my cry.
I felt the solid earth beneath my feet again
and I praised God,
singing a song of joyful thanks.

44

*The friends of Jesus asked him to show them how to pray
and this is what he told them to say.*

Father,
we want everyone to praise you.
We want your Kingdom to grow better and better
until it is perfect.

Give us enough food each day.
Forgive us when we do wrong
—just as we forgive others
    when they do wrong to us.
And help us when we are put to the test.

Listen to Him!

45

God 'speaks' to us in many ways
—he doesn't have to use words.
Sometimes the best way to find out what God our Father
is saying to us is to look around
and see the beauty of his world.

Silently each morning
without a word
without the slightest sound
the golden sun appears
and rises high up in the sky
giving heat and light to everyone.

How beautiful!
How marvellous!

Each day the sky tells all of us
that God is wonderful.

Silently each morning
without a word
without the slightest sound
the sky gives each of us this message
across the whole wide world
as each new day begins.

46

God our Father is the best teacher we can have!

We praise the Lord
for he guides us along the right path.

By day and by night
he shows us what to do.

We shall not fall down
if he is there beside us.

Lord we are happy
for we are safe with you.

47

God our Father is a good teacher.
He wants to show us how to be happy
—happy with each other
—happy with him
—happy in ourselves.
We should listen to him.

Come to me, children.
Listen!
Let me teach you about the Lord.

If you want to be happy,
watch what you say,
don't tell lies,
work for peace.

Taste and see that the Lord is good.

48

*God our Father wants us all
to understand and to be wise.*

Don't be like a donkey
that needs a bridle and a bit,
that turns and runs away
when anyone comes near it.

Be sensible.
Trust God.
HE will teach you what to do.

49

*God our Father wants us to know
that he is gentle and kind.
He will forgive us, if we do wrong.*

God says this

'Come back to me
    and be sorry.
Turn back to me
    for I am gentle.

'I am slow to lose my temper
and very quick to forgive you,
    if you have done wrong.'

50

God our Father wants us to know
that he doesn't like people to be sick and hungry and poor.
He also wants us to know
that he expects us to help him get rid of sickness
and hunger and poverty,
so that the whole world can be full of his goodness and love.

God will remember the poor when they cry.
He will not leave them.
He will take care of the weak and the helpless.

He is loving and kind
and he will remember them.
He will not leave them
crushed down by their enemies.

Blessed be God!
He can work wonders.
Let the whole world be full of his goodness and love!

51

If we want to follow God our Father,
we must listen to him.

We will not do wrong,
we will do what is right.

We will follow God.

We will tell the truth,
we will not tell lies.

We will follow God.

We will be good to our brother,
we will not hurt our neighbour.

We will follow God.

52

Jesus was a great teacher
and many people listened to what he said.
But sometimes he said things in a strange way.
He obviously wanted people to puzzle out what he meant.
He wanted to make them 'think'.
Here are some of the most famous of these puzzling riddles
that Jesus used.

How lucky you are, if you are poor!
God will make you rich!

How lucky you are, if you are not very important!
God will make you great!

How lucky you are, if you are keen to do what *God* wants!
God will see that you get what *you* want as well!

How lucky you are, if you forgive others!
God will forgive you!

How lucky you are, if you really want to know God!
God will make sure you get to know him well!

How lucky you are, if you help people to be friends!
God will be friends with you!

How lucky you are, if people attack you
   especially when you are trying to do what God wants!
God will welcome you with open arms!

Thank Him!

53

God our Father is good and loving.
That's why we thank him.

Let everyone be happy.
Let everyone be glad.
Let everyone be full of joy
and sing to the Lord our God.

We thank you, Lord, we praise you, Lord,
for you are good and loving.

We know the Lord is God.
He gives us life and breath,
for we are his own family,
and we belong to him.

We thank you, Lord, we praise you, Lord,
for you are good and loving.

54

God our Father gives us so much,
we just have to say thank you to him.
It wouldn't be right otherwise!

Thank you, Father,
you are good to us.

You made the sky for us
for you are wise.

Thank you, Father,
you are good to us.

You made the earth for us
for you are kind.

Thank you, Father,
you are good to us.

You gave the sun to us
to shine all day long.

Thank you, Father,
you are good to us.

You gave the moon to us
to shine through the night.

Thank you, Father,
you are good to us.

55

Even plants and animals give thanks to God in their own way!

Let the earth and the sky be glad!
Let the great sea roar!
Let all the fish that swim praise God!
Let the rich green fields be happy!
Let the plants and the animals give thanks to the Lord!
Let the trees in the forest shout for joy!

For God is King. God is King.
He is the Lord of all the world.

56

God our Father is the person who makes this world of ours alive.
That's why we thank him.

You are the one who sends down the early rain
to prepare the soil for the seeds.

You are the one who gathers rain into the rivers
to carry water to the crops.

You are the one who gives us gentle showers
to soak into the hard ploughed fields
to soften the earth
and make the plants sprout and grow.

You are the one who gives us the harvest
filling the valley with golden wheat
and fattening the sheep on the green hillsides.

Let everyone give thanks to you
for all your many blessings,
and sing for joy.

57

God our Father is the Lord of all the world
of the plants and the animals and even the fish.
We thank him for the rich and wonderful world he gives us.

The Lord has blessed the earth once more with rain.
The world has come alive again at last!

Wild donkeys drink
beside the streams of sweet fresh running water,
and birds are building nests up in the trees
singing for joy.

Grass begins to grow again
ready to be eaten by the cattle.
Crops spring up in the farmers' fields
and very soon the olives will ripen on the olive trees.
The harvest is not far away
and then we will enjoy the taste of good new bread.

Little birds are nesting in the cedars,
and storks have settled in the fir trees.
Goats are grazing on the hillsides,
and badgers find a home among the rocks beside the cliffs.

Even the forest animals appear in the shadows of the evening,
and you can hear the lion roaring
hunting for his food throughout the night
until the sun-rise
when the farmer comes out again to work on his fields
and the lion returns into his den.

And that's not all!
In the waters of the Ocean
countless fish both large and small swim here and there,
and whales and sharks dive and play in the depths below.

. . . and every one of these depend on you for life!
If you should turn away,
they would be helpless.
If you did not breathe life into their lungs
they would just die!
That is why you give them food
and they are satisfied.

Lord God, the world is full of good things you have made.
How wonderful you are!
How wise!

58

You could imagine the blind man
who was cured by Jesus saying his prayer.

I love you, my Lord,
for you have made me strong.

I thank you, my Lord,
for you have heard my prayer.

You have been like a light before my eyes.
You have made my darkness into light.

I thank you, my Lord,
for you have heard my prayer.

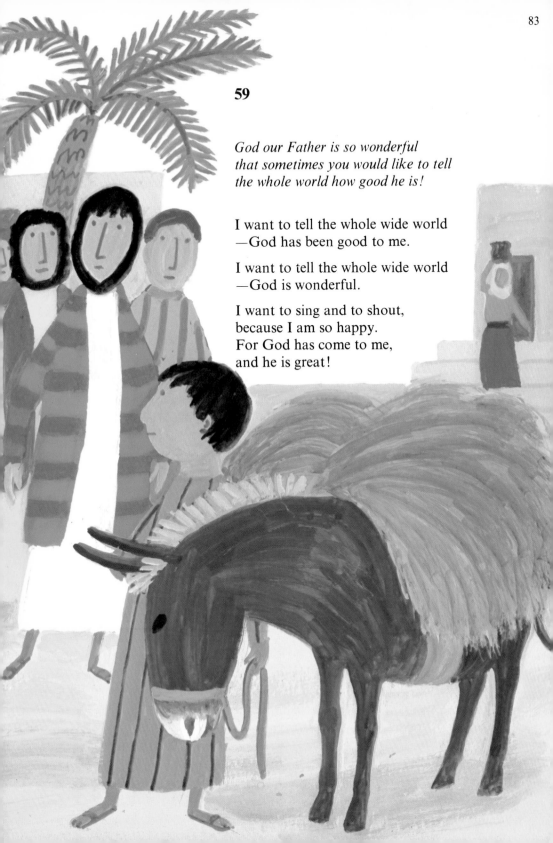

59

*God our Father is so wonderful
that sometimes you would like to tell
the whole world how good he is!*

I want to tell the whole wide world
—God has been good to me.

I want to tell the whole wide world
—God is wonderful.

I want to sing and to shout,
because I am so happy.
For God has come to me,
and he is great!

60

God our Father loves us
—he loves us in the same way as he loves his Son, Jesus
for we also are his children!
That's why we say 'thank you' to him.

Give thanks to God the Father.
He has made us brothers of Christ!

Even before the world was made,
he chose us to be his very own people
—the People of Christ.

He wanted us to live like him
—in goodness and friendship,
for he had decided that we should be his own children.

He loved us so much
that he wanted us to be his sons and daughters.

LET US PRAISE GOD!

A NOTE FOR PARENTS AND TEACHERS
ON THE CHOICE AND THE TRANSLATION
OF THESE TEXTS

The psalms and the canticles were never specifically intended to be read or listened to as children's verse. Perhaps it is necessary, therefore, to give some explanation of why this collection of songs and prayers from the Old and New Testament has been put together in a form specially directed towards young children.

The Book of Psalms has often been called 'the prayerbook of the Old Testament'. It is, in fact, a collection of ancient Hebrew poems and songs gathered together for liturgical use. Like many prayerbooks it is adult in tone and largely concerned with adult problems. On the other hand it is more varied than many other collections, since it reflects the feelings and experiences of almost the whole 'lifetime' of the ancient people of Israel.

It is important to realise that the individual psalms (and also the later canticles and poems modelled on them) are ancient texts with all the strangeness and obscurity of documents of long ago. They are written in a style quite different from the poems and songs of today. Yet not completely so—many people have found that they speak with a directness and a vividness which can be very attractive to the modern reader. The response to the much smaller selection of psalms given in my earlier volume of biblical readings has encouraged me to think they can be equally attractive to the younger reader.

As in the earlier *Listen!*, I have tried to pick out those passages most appealing to young children, and to present them as far as possible in the language of the children themselves. This has been done both to help children here and now in their prayers to God and to introduce them to the full collection of the psalms which, hopefully, they will use as adults. Usually this has meant giving only a portion of an individual psalm. Frequently a single metaphor or simile has been allowed to dominate an individual 'poem', even when it was only one of several employed in the original. Few adults are completely at ease today with the formal patterns of ancient semitic poetry. It is hardly surprising if young children find themselves faced with similar difficulties. This collection merely tries to draw their attention to some of the good things that can be overlooked when they are 'lost' in the text.

However, in one way a child can be in a more privileged position than those older than himself when he comes to read or listen to these prayers from long ago. The psalms speak with great immediacy of happiness, sadness, anger, gratitude and trust in a manner that can at times be more intelligible to a child than an adult. All the more

A NOTE FOR PARENTS AND TEACHERS

reason, then, for presenting these rich and imaginative poems in an approachable manner.

The more one ponders over the psalms in all their variety the more one hesitates to leave out any of them even from a collection like this. But in practice it was impossible for me to provide an adequate version of all 150 psalms. No doubt some of those which have been omitted will be among other people's favourites. The reasons for individual omissions obviously vary. Sometimes a well-known psalm will have been left out simply because it too closely duplicates material already given elsewhere. Sometimes it will have been left out because it is one of those 'difficult' texts which could not be included in full, and the attractive image contained in it was too precisely 'tied up' in the general argument of the full psalm to be presented on its own—even the most telling of images cannot fairly be taken out of its context without being allowed to express in some way the meaning for which it was chosen. Even so, I would suggest most aspects of the psalms and the canticles are represented here in spite of the many omissions.

No attempt has been made to 'poeticise' or metricalise these versions of the psalms. In the originals it is usual to find individual lines divided in two, each half reflecting the meaning of the other in a kind of parallel.[1] I hope this point of style is expressed in the present version—though often it is to be found more in the use of a succession of similar lines than in the internal 'shape' of individual lines.

As in *Listen!* I have made use of a careful division of the text into sense lines in order to assist the young reader to read the poems out loud intelligently, rather than to make the text 'look' like modern poetry.

Also as in *Listen!*, the psalms have been numbered throughout according to the Grail edition (Collins 1963)—though I must admit that I have not always followed the Grail interpretation of the individual texts.

[1]This is reflected in many modern translations very clearly, and especially in the 'Grail' edition.

BRIEF TEXTS FROM THE GOSPELS

Many of these psalms provide a colourful illustration or commentary on the words and actions of Christ in the Gospels. The following brief texts are provided as examples of relevant quotations for use in a school or church situation where it is desirable to follow the psalm with a specific reference to the life of Christ. These short passages could also provide a Gospel reading for use in a simple liturgy of the word. Generally speaking they have been kept as close as possible to the wording of standard modern translations (except for those employing the words of the Lord's Prayer) so that they may more easily be recognised as 'words of Christ' in spite of their brevity.

1   Jesus said 'Father, I want to share my joy to the full with all those you have given to me' (John 17:13).
2   Jesus said this prayer 'Our Father, who art in heaven, hallowed be thy name' (Matthew 6:10).
3   Jesus said 'Be sure your Father in heaven will give good things to those who ask him' (Matthew 7:11).
4   Jesus said 'I have come so that you may have life and have it to the full' (John 10:10).
or   Jesus said 'A sound tree produces good fruit' (Matthew 7:17).
5   Jesus said 'Father, all that I have is yours' (John 17:10).
6   *See* 5.
7   Jesus said 'I am with you always, yes to the end of time' (Matthew 28:20).
8   Jesus said 'I call you friends' (John 17:15).
9   Jesus exclaimed 'I bless you, Father, you are Lord of heaven and earth' (Matthew 11:25—'bless' here means 'give thanks').
10   Jesus said 'Where two or three are gathered together in my name, I am there with them' (Matthew 18:20).
11   Simon Peter said 'Lord, you have the message of eternal life and we believe. We know you are the Holy One of God' (John 6:68).
12   Jesus said 'You did not choose me. I chose you' (John 15:16).
13   The messenger from God said to Mary 'Do not be afraid. You will give birth to a son. He will be great and God will make him king like David long ago. He will rule over his people for ever' (Luke 1:31–33).
14   Jesus said 'I am the vine, you are the branches. Whoever remains in me, bears fruit in plenty' (John 15:5).
15   Jesus said 'Unless a wheat germ falls on the ground and dies, it remains a single grain. But if it dies, it yields a rich harvest' (John 12:24).
16   Jesus said 'My house shall be a house of prayer for all the peoples' (Mark 11:17).
17   This is a Gospel text.

18 Jesus said 'Father I thank you for hearing my prayer. I know you always hear me' (John 11:42).

19 Jesus said 'Peace be with you' and his disciples were filled with joy (John 20:20).

20 Jesus said 'If your faith were the size of a mustard seed, nothing would be impossible for you' (Matthew 17:20).

21 The power of God was behind the works of Jesus . . . and the people were all astounded and praised God, and were filled with awe (Luke 5:17–26—the healing of the paralytic reveals the gentle strength of Christ).

22 Jesus said 'You will see the Son of Man coming on the clouds of heaven with power and great glory. The great trumpet will sound and he will send out his messengers to the four corners of the earth and they will gather his chosen people from one end of the earth to the other' (Matthew 24:30–31).

23 Jesus said to the blind man 'Receive your sight' and immediately his sight returned and he followed him praising God. And all the people who saw it gave praise to God (Luke 18:42–43).

24 Jesus said 'Do you not understand? Are your minds closed? Have you eyes that do not see and ears that do not hear?' (Mark 8:17–18).

25 Jesus said 'Why do you call me "Lord, Lord" and do not do what I say?' (Luke 6:46).

26 Jesus said 'Come to me, all you who are over-burdened and I will give you rest' (Matthew 11:28–29).

27 Jesus said 'Do not be afraid: every hair on your head has been counted' (Matthew 10:30–31).

28 This is a Gospel text.

29 Jesus said 'As the Father has loved me so I have loved you. Remain in my love' (John 15:9).

30 Jesus said this prayer 'Father, lead us not into temptation' (Matthew 6–13—the real temptation is to trust in things, not in God).

31 *See* 36.

32 Jesus said 'Do not let your hearts be troubled. Trust in God still and trust in me' (John 14:1).

33 Jesus said 'I am the good shepherd. I know my own and my own know me' (John 10:14).

34 Jesus said 'Do not worry about your life. God will look after you. Your Father knows what you need. There is no need to be afraid' (Luke 12:22, 28–33).

35 Jesus said 'In this world you will have trouble. But be brave: I have overcome the world' (John 16:33).

36 One day Jesus got into a boat with his disciples. Then without warning a storm broke over the lake so violent that the waves were breaking right over the boat. But Jesus was asleep. So his

disciples went to him and woke him, saying 'Save us, Lord' (Matthew 8:23–25).

37 Jesus said 'I tell you—although you will have sorrow, your sorrow will turn to joy' (John 16:20).

38 Jesus said 'Whoever comes to me I will not turn him away' (John 6:37).

39 Jesus said 'Ask and you will receive, and your joy will be complete' (John 16:24).

40 Jesus said this prayer 'Father, deliver us from evil' (Matthew 6:13).

41 Jesus said to Zaccheus 'Hurry, I must stay in your house today.' And Zaccheus welcomed him joyfully. Jesus said 'I have come to seek out and save what was lost' (Luke 16:5, 6–10).

42 The people said 'Take him away, take him away. Crucify him' . . . When the soldiers had finished crucifying Jesus, they took his clothing and divided it into four shares . . . Jesus said 'I am thirsty' and bowing his head he gave up the spirit . . . (John 19:15–30).

43 Jesus came to the disciples walking on the lake. So Peter got out of the boat and started walking towards him across the water. As soon as he felt the force of the wind, he took fright and began to sink. But Jesus put out his hand at once and held him (Matthew 14:25–31).

44 This is a Gospel text.

45 Jesus said 'See how our Father in heaven causes the sun to shine on bad men as well as good' (Matthew 5:45).

46 Jesus said 'I, the Light, have come into the world so that whoever believes in me need not stay in the dark any more' (John 12:46).

47 Jesus said 'I give you a new commandment: Love one another. Just as I have loved you, you must love one another' (John 13:34).

48 Jesus said this prayer 'Father, thy will be done on earth as it is in heaven' (Matthew 6:10).

49 Jesus said this prayer 'Father, forgive us our trespasses as we forgive those who trespass against us' (Matthew 6:12).

50 Jesus said 'I was hungry, and you gave me food. I was thirsty, and you gave me drink. I was a stranger, and you made me welcome. I was naked, and you clothed me. I was sick, and you visited me' (Matthew 25:35).

51 Jesus said 'Treat others as you would like them to treat you' (Luke 6:31).

52 This is a Gospel text.

53 Jesus said 'If you keep my commandments, you will remain in my love. I have told you this so that my own joy may be in you and your joy be complete' (John 15:10–11).

54 Jesus is 'a light that shines in the dark, a light that darkness could not overpower' (John 1:5).

55 Jesus said 'Think of the wild flowers. I tell you not even Solomon as rich as he was had clothes as beautiful as one of these flowers' (Matthew 6:28–29).

56 Jesus said 'Some seed fell into rich soil and, growing strong and tall, produced crop and yielded thirty, sixty, even a hundred fold' (Mark 4:8).

57 Jesus said this prayer 'Father, thy kingdom come' (Matthew 6:10 —the kingdom is filled with the goodness, richness and life that comes from God).

58 Jesus said 'I am the light of the world. Anyone who follows me will not be walking in the dark. He will have the light of life' (John 8:12).

59 Jesus said 'How happy are you to see what you see' (Luke 10:23— i.e. because the disciples have seen Jesus himself).

60 Jesus said 'Father, I pray that they may all be one as we are one' (John 17:22).

RESPONSES FOR USE WITH THE TEXTS

The psalms were composed for many different types of situations and they follow a variety of styles and forms. There is a similar variety provided in the texts presented in this volume, with some given in the form of chants with refrains, others as narrative poems, and yet others as short meditations.

As they stand, therefore, not all of them are suitable as responsorial psalms for use in acts of worship with children. Nevertheless Christians have long used most of the psalms in this way by providing them with responses, and the following notes show how these texts also could be turned into responsorial psalms by the addition of suitable refrains. Where a response comes after an irregular number of lines, it may be necessary for the reader to say it on each occasion so that the rest of the children can repeat it.

Praise him!

1 *God is king of all the earth* may be used as a response throughout.

2 *Let everyone praise God* may be used as a response throughout.

3 *Our God is powerful, our God is wise. Praise him!* may be used as a response throughout.

4 *Give praise to God* may be used as a response at the beginning and end of this text and after each verse.

5   *Blessed be God* may be used as a response throughout.
6   *Everything you do, O Lord, is strange and marvellous* may be used as a response throughout.
7   *You are always close to me. You're wonderful, O Lord* may be used as a response throughout.
8   *You are so great, O Lord* may be used as a response at the beginning and end of the text.
9   *Blessed be God* may be used as a response throughout.
10   *Let's praise him* may be used as a response throughout with everyone joining together for the last two lines as well.
11   *You are the king of the whole wide world* may be used as a response after each verse.

Remember him!

12   This long narrative poem is not easily made into a responsorial psalm. However it may be made to sound more effective by being divided into two alternating sections for choral recitation, with group A reading stanzas 2, 4, 6, 8 and group B reading stanzas 3, 5, 7, 9. Both groups should join together to say the opening lines and the last two lines.
     Give thanks to the Lord or *Remember the goodness of God* may be used as responses when only a shorter portion of the text is to be used.
13   *Lord remember us and give us your help* may be used as a response throughout.
14   *Take care of us, Lord* may be introduced as a response after each verse.
15   *In good times and bad times we can always trust God* may be used as a response throughout.
16   *Lord God, I put my trust in you* may be used as a response throughout.
17   *Praise the Lord for he has visited his people* may be used as a response throughout.

Get to know him!

18   *Blessed be God* may be used as a response throughout.
19   *You are our God* may be used as a response throughout.
20   *Lord God I am happy to be with you* may be used as a response throughout.
21   *Glory to God in the highest* may be used as a response throughout.
22   *Lord God, how great you are* or *Blessed be God* or *Glory to God in the highest* may be used as a response throughout.
23   See no. 22 for suitable responses.
24   This poem is not easily made into a responsorial psalm. But it can be made to sound more effective when read aloud if different

children/groups of children say alternate lines and then join together for the last two lines.

25 This poem is not easily made into a responsorial psalm. But it can be made to sound more effective when different children/groups of children read each of the stanzas.

26 *In good times or bad times we can always trust God* may be used as a response throughout. But this poem is really too personal to be easily made into a responsorial psalm and sounds more effective if read by three different readers, one for each stanza.

27 It is not easy to find a response which fits both halves of this psalm. But the words *Lord God our Father, we will stay close to you* may be introduced after each of the three main verses of the second half.

28 *I praise the Lord for he is good* may be used as a response throughout.

Trust him!

29 *I trust in God* may be used as a response throughout.

30 *God will take care of us* may be used as a response at the beginning and end and between each stanza.

31 *In good times and bad times we can always trust God* may be used as a response throughout.

32 It is not easy to find a response which fits both halves of this psalm. But the words *Lord listen to my prayer* may be introduced after each of the four verses of the second half.

33 *The Lord is our shepherd, he takes good care of us* may be used as a response throughout.

34 *Lord, I am safe with you* may be used as a response throughout.

35 *Lord, I put my trust in you* may be used as a response throughout.

Ask him!

36 *Lord, come and help us now* may be used as a response throughout.

37 This is not a poem that can be easily made into a responsorial psalm and is best left as it is.

38 *Listen to my cry for help, O Lord* may be used as a response throughout.

39 *Lord God you are my strength* may be used as a response throughout.

40 *Save me, O Lord* may be used as a response throughout.

41 *Forgive me, Lord* may be used as a response throughout.

42 *Lord, come and help me* may be used as a response throughout. Alternatively, the text may be used without a response, with each verse read by a different child, who then read in unison for the last verse.

43   It is not easy to find a response that fits both verses of this text. Possibly two responses could be provided: *Help me Lord* might be said after the first verse, and *Praise the Lord* after the second.

44   This text is really too short and concise to be turned into a responsorial 'psalm' and should be left as it is.

Listen to him!

45   *Lord God, how great you are* may be used as a response throughout.

46   *Lord God, we are safe with you* may be used as a response throughout.

47   *Taste and see that the Lord is good* may be used as a response throughout.

48   *The Lord will teach us what to do* may be used as a response throughout.

49   *The Lord is gentle and forgiving* may be used as a response throughout.

50   *Never forget what the Lord has done* may be used as a response throughout.

51   *We will follow God* may be used as a response throughout.

52   This text can be made to sound more effective by giving each of the 'beatitudes' to a different reader.

Thank him!

53   *We thank you, Lord, we praise you, Lord, for you are good and loving* may be used as a response throughout.

54   *Thank you, Father, you are good to us* may be used as a response.

55   It is not easy to introduce one simple response into this text, but at least the last two lines may be repeated by all the children.

56   *Sing and shout with joy for God is great* may be used as a response throughout.

57   *Lord, how wonderful you are, how wise* may be used as a response if necessary. But this text is not easily made into a responsorial psalm and is better read by several readers each taking a separate verse. This is also a psalm that can be mimed to great effect.

58   *I thank you, my Lord, for you have heard my prayer* may be used as a response throughout.

59   The last line of each verse may be repeated in this psalm, i.e. *God has been good to me/God is wonderful/God is great.*

60   *Let us praise God* may be used as a response throughout.

WHERE TO FIND THESE TEXTS IN YOUR BIBLE

WHERE TO FIND PASSAGES FROM THE BIBLE IN THIS BOOK

Old Testament

New Testament